Discovering Our Jewish Roots

A Simple Guide to Judaism

Anna Marie Erst, S.H.C.J.

PAULIST PRESS
New York/Mahwah, N.J.

Special thanks and acknowledgments are made for the contributions of Judith Banki, who wrote the text of Chapter 3, which was then reviewed and accepted by the author of the book, Anna Marie Erst. Ms. Banki also reviewed other parts of the manuscript and offered suggestions for various sections. Ms. Banki is a writer, lecturer, and acknowledged expert in interreligious affairs. Her writings and research reports have largely focused on two central aspects of the Jewish-Christian encounter: the image of the Jews in Christian teaching and preaching, and Christian church attitudes toward the State of Israel. She served for more than thirty years as Associate National Director of Interreligious Affairs for The American Jewish Committee and as editor of the *Interreligious Newsletter*.

Cover design by Jim Brisson.

Library of Congress Cataloging-in-Publication Data

Erst, Anna Marie.
   Discovering our Jewish roots : a simple guide to Judaism / by Anna Marie Erst.
      p. cm.
   Includes bibliographical references.
   ISBN 0-8091-3654-6 (alk. paper)
   1. Judaism. 2. Judaism–Relations–Christianity. 3. Christianity and other religions–Judaism. I. Title.
BM582.E77 1996
296–dc20   96-9302
                                             CIP

Published by Paulist Press
997 Macarthur Boulevard
Mahwah, New Jersey 07430

Printed and bound in the
United States of America

Contents

Foreword

Jesus of Nazareth lived and died as a believing Jew. Moreover, as the church historian Franklin Littell has compellingly reminded us, if Jesus had been alive during the time when the Nazis were exterminating Jews in Europe, he would have very likely been taken away to the crematoria with his people. Yet many Christians have been conditioned to regard Jesus as essentially anti-Jewish in the fundamentals of his teaching and preaching. Certainly Jesus (along with other Jewish leaders of the day) disagreed with many of the approaches to belief and practice promoted by certain Jewish groups of the time such as the Sadducees. He likewise questioned some of the policies of the Temple priests in Jerusalem, carrying his protest to the point of dramatic confrontation when he invaded the Temple precincts to remove the money changers who were then an integral part of the Temple system. While few other Jewish leaders of the time were prepared to state publicly their criticism of the Temple system and its priestly leaders in as bold a fashion as Jesus, they stood with him in terms of a general commitment to a major renewal of religious life and practice.

Recently, church documents, ecclesial leaders and individual scholars have begun to reemphasize Jesus' deep roots in the Judaism of his day, especially his ties with the forces

1

involved with the wholesale renewal of Jewish life. The 1985 Vatican notes on teaching and preaching about Jews and Judaism in Catholicism tell us that "Jesus was and always remained a Jew....Jesus is fully a man of his time and his environment—the Jewish Palestinian one of the first century, the anxieties and hope of which he shared" (see Helga Croner, ed., *More Stepping Stones to Jewish-Christian Relations* [New York: Paulist Press, A Stimulus Book, 1985], 226). And Cardinal Carlo Martini of Milan, a noted biblical scholar, has made much the same point: "In its origins Christianity is deeply rooted in Judaism. Without a sincere feeling for the Jewish world, therefore, and a direct experience of it, one cannot understand Christianity. Jesus is fully Jewish, the apostles are Jewish, and one cannot doubt their attachment to the traditions of their forefathers" (see James H. Charlesworth, ed., *Jews and Christians: Exploring the Past, Present, and Future* [New York: Crossroad, 1990], 19).

This new understanding of the Jewish-Christian relationship at its origins supplants the long-held view in Christianity that the church displaced the Jewish people in the fundamental covenantal relationship with the Creator God because they had rejected Jesus as the Messiah. As a result of their displacement from the covenant, many prominent church fathers argued that the Jews were to be perpetual wanderers among the peoples of the earth without a homeland of their own as a sign of their reprobation and as a continual warning to people of the dangers of rejecting Jesus.

This teaching, which in fact has little or no basis in the New Testament, along with equally distorted views of Jewish responsibility for the crucifixion and death of Jesus and of the Jewish renewal movement called Pharisaism, became the basis of Christian theology and catechesis for centuries. As the St. Louis textbook studies undertaken in the late fifties and early sixties at St. Louis University (see John T. Pawlikowski, *Catechetics & Prejudice* [New York: Paulist

Press, 1973]) clearly show, these distorted views of Jews and Judaism were still very apparent at the dawn of Vatican II. The subsequent studies on Catholic teaching materials by Dr. Eugene J. Fisher in the seventies (*Faith Without Prejudice* [New York: Paulist Press, 1977] and Dr. Philip Cunningham in the nineties (*Education for Shalom* [Collegeville, Minn. Liturgical Press, 1994]) definitely showed marked improvement in the presentation of Jews and Judaism. But the classical stereotypes have not completely vanished, not even in the materials recently surveyed by Cunningham.

In light of the revolutionary change that has occurred in Christian scholarship and church teaching regarding Christianity's relationship with Judaism, Sister Anna Marie Erst's *Discovering Our Jewish Roots* is especially welcome. There are many texts now available that introduce Christian students to the history of the Christian-Jewish relationship. These texts are surely important as a counter to the distorted presentations of the past that still retain a foothold in sectors of popular Christian faith. But there are very few texts that present the basics of Jewish belief in the clear, readable way that this volume does.

As Cardinal Martini has insisted, unless we come to understand Judaism and, in the words of the 1974 Vatican guidelines, come to understand it as Jews themselves interpret it, we cannot fully grasp the message of Jesus and early Christianity. Basic Christian beliefs are strongly linked to prevailing Jewish ideas about God, religious leadership, ethics, worship, and the structure of the religious assembly. There are also important links between Jewish festivals and subsequent Christian liturgical celebrations. All this points to the theme that Pope John Paul II has stressed in a number of his public addresses, including his historic visit to the Rome synagogue: Jews and Christians are linked together in a most intimate way, in fact, at the very basic level of their self-identity.

Sister Anna Marie's new volume both exemplifies the new spirit of the Christian-Jewish encounter and provides the basic knowledge students need to forge the new identity that John Paul II has underlined as central to Catholic faith today. It deserves a warm welcome as an invaluable instructional aid from teachers and pastoral leaders.

(Rev.) John T. Pawlikowski, O.S.M., Ph.D.
Professor,
Catholic Theological Union,
Chicago, Ill.

Member, Executive Committee,
U.S. Holocaust Memorial Council

Member,
Advisory Committee on Catholic-Jewish Relations,
National Council of Catholic Bishops

Chapter 1

Why Study Judaism?

Why? Because Jesus was a Jew. He studied the *Torah* (the first five books of the Bible) and lived a thoroughly Jewish life following the traditions and teachings of his people, the Jews of Palestine. Many of his teachings and his method of teaching were in accord with those of Judaism. Many Catholic theologians claim that 80 percent to 85 percent of what Christians believe comes from the Judaic religion. We are enriched by the study of Judaism, and we gain a deeper understanding of our own religion.

WHO WERE THESE JEWS FROM WHOM JESUS DESCENDED?

They were a people to whom God revealed himself. To them he gave the task of making known to the world the one true God. Because of this the Jews are often referred to as the "chosen people"—chosen by God for a definite work. God emphasized this bond with the Jewish people by establishing a covenant on Mount Sinai through Moses. To Moses God gave the tablets of the law: the Ten Commandments. Obeying these laws in a totally pagan world caused the Jews to be considered the "different people."

WHY THE DIFFERENT PEOPLE?

In ancient pagan times the Jews were considered different. They refused to worship the pagan gods. They refused to take part in pagan festivals. They refused to work on the Sabbath day, even when punished for this refusal. They even refused to allow their servants to work on the Sabbath. The Sabbath was the seventh day of the week, a day that God commanded them to keep holy. They were to spend time reading the Torah, to avoid all unnecessary labor, and to enjoy the companionship of family and friends. It was a day to renew one's self spiritually and physically—a most important, most sacred, and joyous day.

Furthermore, the Jews followed strict dietary laws that prevented them from socializing with their pagan neighbors because they were afraid of being given non-kosher food to eat. The dietary laws required that animals be slaughtered in as painless a way as possible and that meat and dairy products not be served at the same time, among other things. The dietary laws were rooted in the Torah. As a result, the Jews' lives were often made miserable. They were persecuted and even put to death.

CHRISTIAN-JEWISH RELATIONS THROUGH THE CENTURIES

The first followers of Jesus were members of the Jewish community. They worshiped in the Temple and synagogues, kept the Jewish laws and traditions, and associated with the other Jews. Then why did trouble occur between Jesus' Jewish followers and the other Jews? One of the reasons was the conversion of non-Jews to the teachings of Jesus. These non-Jews (Gentiles) brought with them the anti-Jewish stereotypes they already had. Other reasons were the tension, disputes, and mutual rejection between the Jews who believed in Jesus and the Jews who did not. Some Christian leaders accused the

Jews of putting Jesus to death (known as the deicide charge). Despite efforts made by the Christian churches to counteract this charge, some people, even today, believe the Jews were responsible for Jesus' death.

There were times of peaceful coexistence and even cooperation between Christians and Jews down through the centuries, but there also were many times of tension resulting in shameful treatment of the Jews. Restrictions were placed upon the Jews. They were barred from most sectors of civic, social, professional, and commercial life. In A.D. 1215, Pope Innocent III, fearing that Jews might contaminate Christians, decreed that Jews must wear a "badge of shame" in Christian lands. No Jew could own a Christian slave, though Christians could own Jewish slaves. No Jew could testify against a Christian in court. Since Christians were forbidden to lend money at interest to each other, the Jews were allowed to do so, but often the money was confiscated by Christian overlords. Yet Christians in thought and in literature created the stereotype of the Jew as money-hungry and power-hungry. During the Crusades, the Jews were labeled the "infidels at home." Whole villages of Jews were wiped out; money owed to Jews by Christians was given to fund the Crusades.

Even when Jews retaliated, the Christians usually won because they had the power. The Jews were blamed for any catastrophes that occurred. They were the scapegoats. They were massacred, burned alive, drowned in rivers. This shameful treatment (which was unchristian as much as it was anti-Jewish) did much to make the holocaust possible in World War II. Prejudice and degrading stereotypes that are allowed to grow unchecked will lead to uncalled for, tragic, unjust suffering.

HOPE FOR THE FUTURE

It is especially important that we Christians make every effort to understand, accept, and respect the Jewish people.

We owe them so much, yet they have suffered much from misguided Christians. We cannot excuse what Christians have done. Our task is to see that, as far as it is in our power, such atrocities never again occur. We must take care to avoid mistaking human failings for racial or national characteristics, and condemning a group for what a few have done.

The horrors of the holocaust awakened Christian consciences. In 1948, the World Council of Churches issued a statement condemning anti-Semitism (the term commonly used for anti-Jewishness). In its Third Assembly, meeting in New Delhi, India, in 1961, the Council recalled the 1948 statement:

> We call upon all churches we represent to denounce anti-Semitism, no matter what its origin, as absolutely irreconcilable with the profession and practice of the Christian faith. Anti-Semitism is a sin against God and man....
>
> The Assembly (1961) renews this plea...and urges its member churches to do all in their power to resist every form of anti-Semitism.

In recent years, a number of Protestant denominations and groups have not only condemned anti-Semitism, but also have begun to establish friendly relationships with the Jewish people.

In 1965, the bishops of the Roman Catholic Church, meeting in Rome at Vatican Council II, published the document *Nostra Aetate (In Our Times),* part IV of which deals with the church's relationship with the Jews:

> The Church repudiates all persecutions against any person. Moreover, mindful of her common patrimony with the Jews, and motivated by the gospel's spiritual love and by no political considerations, she deplores the hatred, persecutions, and displays of anti-Semitism directed against the Jews at any time and from any source.

In the "Notes on the Correct Way to Present Jews and Judaism in Preaching and Catechesis in the Roman Catholic Church" (1995), clarifying the council document, the church states that "the Jews are to be *presented as the 'people of God of the Old Testament, which has never been revoked by God, and as the Chosen People.'*"

Three recent events reflect the great strides that have been made in Catholic-Jewish relations:

– On December 30, 1993, Pope John Paul II and Ezer Weizman, the president of Israel, established diplomatic relations between the Holy See and Israel. Archbishop Montezemolo was designated the first Vatican diplomat to Israel, and some months later, Shmuel Hadas was designated the first ambassador of Israel to the Holy See. The Holy Father said he hoped this extraordinary step would lead to the fulfillment of his dream: *"I dream of the day when Jews, Christians and Muslims will salute each other in Jerusalem with the greeting of peace."*

– In April 1994, the Holy Father hosted a program in commemoration of the holocaust that was held in the large audience hall in the Vatican. The Chief Rabbi of Rome, several other rabbis, a number of cardinals and bishops, and hundreds of priests, members of religious congregations, and laypeople attended the program. It was televised and highly acclaimed by all who saw it.

– Very recently—in March 1995—Joseph Cardinal Bernardin, archbishop of Chicago, led an interfaith group to Israel; he was the first high-ranking prelate to do so. While in Jerusalem, he made two statements of great importance for Christian-Jewish relations: The cardinal urged a restoration of the history of Christian anti-Semitism and anti-Judaic theology to Catholic education. He said, too: *"including this history, as painful as it is for us today, is*

> *a necessary requirement for authentic reconciliation between Christians in our time."*

The other statement of importance was: *"Above all, in light of the anti-Semitism and the holocaust, the Church needs to engage in public repentance."*

Since Vatican II, every Catholic diocese has an office of ecumenical and interfaith relations whose work is to help its people to learn to know, accept, and respect the beliefs, traditions, and rites of non-Catholics. Every member of the human race belongs to the all-embracing family of God. All who believe in God have the same goals: to make the one, true God known, and to build his kingdom on earth. If we could but learn to join hands and work together, just think of what our world could be!

Torah scroll

Chapter 2

Learning the Language of Judaism

Before entering on our brief study of Judaism, it may be of help to explain the terms you will find in the material that may not be explained in the text. The spelling of Hebrew words may differ in other books or articles, but usually they are recognizable: for example, Hanukkah, Hannukah, Chanukah, or yad, yod.

afikomen (from the Greek, meaning "dessert"). The half of the middle matzoh that is hidden during the Passover meal. When found by the children at the end of the meal, it is shared by all present. No food is served after eating the piece of matzoh, though wine may be served.

blintzes. Thin pancakes on which favorite fillings are spread, then rolled and lightly sprinkled with powdered sugar. Fresh fruit may garnish the pancakes.

cantor. The one who chants or sings the Hebrew texts at synagogue services. Women may be cantors in all but the Orthodox Congregations, which include the Hasidim.

citron (etrog). A lemon-like fruit from the Holy Land used during the Sukkot holiday.

havdalah candle. A braided candle with two or more wicks that is lighted after sunset on the Sabbath to mark the end of the Sabbath. *Havdalah* means "set aside," referring to God's separation of the Sabbath from the other days of the week. Lighting a fire or candle is not permitted on the Sabbath, so the lighting of the havdalah candle is done after sunset. It is braided (using two or more thin candles) because the blessings of the Sabbath should permeate the entire week.

Kiddush cup. *Kiddush* means "sanctification." The cup, which is often very ornate, is used for the cup of wine over which the traditional benediction and prayer is said on the Sabbath and on feasts. This cup is comparable to the chalice used by priests in the mass.

kosher. Refers to foods used and prepared in accordance with Jewish law. Animals that have cloven hooves and chew their cud, birds that are not birds of prey, and fish that have fins and scales are approved foods. All animals, birds, and fish must be killed in the manner that is least painful. Meats must be thoroughly soaked to rid them of all blood, then salted and, after an hour, thoroughly rinsed before being cooked. Some Jews, especially Orthodox Jews, keep dairy and meat products—and the plates and utensils used to serve them—completely separate. *Kosher,* which means "fit," can refer to anything that is done or made in accordance with Jewish law.

lulav. A palm branch with a few sprigs of myrtle and willow used during the Sukkot holiday.

matzoh. The cracker-like, unleavened bread used by Jews during the Passover season. No leavened bread is eaten during the eight days of Passover. This serves as a reminder of the haste with which the Israelites had to flee from Egypt. There was no time to wait for the dough to rise.

mezuzah. A small scroll on which is written two extracts from Deuteronomy (6:4-9 and 11:13-21) that command the Jews to love God and obey his commandments. On the reverse side of the scroll is printed the word *Shaddai,* meaning "Almighty." The scroll is placed in a case, which may be simple or ornate. The term *mezuzah* commonly refers to the scroll and its case. No definite directions are given for the appearance or material of the case, but its placement is definitely stated:

1. It should be on the doorposts of all permanent dwellings.
2. It should be fastened to the upper third of the right doorpost.
3. It should slant toward the room being entered.
4. The scroll is to be hand-printed in Hebrew—a very difficult task since the scroll is only two inches by two inches, requiring very tiny letters. Today, commercially printed scrolls are used by many Jews. Some Jews attach mezuzahs on the doorposts of every room used as a dwelling. The Jews touch the mezuzah with their fingers as they enter. It reminds them of God and his commandments. To visitors, it indicates that the Jewish family follows God's law.

phylacteries (tefillin). The small, black leather-covered boxes, with long leather, ribbon-like straps that Jewish men don for morning prayer, except on the Sabbath and holy days. The boxes contain parchment scrolls on which prescribed passages from the Torah are hand-printed in Hebrew. On the surface of the boxes are Hebrew letters that stand for *Shaddai,* meaning "Almighty," referring to God. One box is placed on the upper left arm, facing the heart. The leather strap is wound around the left arm seven times in a distinct, orderly fashion. The other box is placed on the forehead between and above the eyes. Its strap is wound around the head to hold the box in place.

prayer shawl (tallit). A long, rectangular piece of silk or wool with a few black or blue stripes on each end and knotted fringes at the four corners. The knotted fringes, called *tzitzit,* should remind the wearer of the commandments. The prayer shawl is worn by men at morning prayer and all prayer services on Yom Kippur. Orthodox Jews reserve the wearing of the prayer shawl to married men. Often the prayer said when putting on the prayer shawl is embroidered as a collar on the part of the shawl that covers the neck, head, or shoulders.

rabbi (meaning "my teacher"). A rabbi is a recognized leader of a given community, a competent authority on Jewish law. Rabbis have always been men until recently. Today, women may be rabbis in most Jewish communities, but never in Orthodox (which includes the Hasidim) communities.

shofar. Usually a ram's horn, but it may be the horn of any male animal. It gives forth a loud, sharp tone and is very difficult to "play." It was used to assemble the people, to warn of danger, to welcome the new year, and to enhance such ceremonies as the coronation of a king. Today, its principal use is at the morning service of Rosh Hashanah and to announce the end of the fast on Yom Kippur.

spice box. A container for precious spices. It has no specific size or shape, except that it should have some perforations to enable the perfume of the spices to be inhaled. The spice box is used in the havdalah service after sundown at the close of the Sabbath.

Star of David

Star of David. A six-pointed star, sometimes called the *Magen David,* meaning "shield of David." It is said to have been the symbol on David's coat of arms, his sword, etc. The Star of David has been a popular Jewish symbol since the nineteenth century. It is woven on the pall covering the sarcophagus of David's tomb in Jerusalem. The Star of David is also on the State of Israel's flag.

synagogue. The name given to the building or buildings used by a Jewish community for worship services, meetings, study, social events, etc. Synagogues vary in size and shape. The basic rules are simply that the sanctuary (prayer room) should have an ark in the east wall to hold the Torah, a platform from which the Torah is read, and windows, and should not be too ostentatious. An atmosphere of holiness should prevail. Many synagogues also have an office for the rabbi, a library, classrooms for the students, and a large meeting room with an adjoining kitchen for meetings, concerts, social events, etc. In large and very active synagogues, offices and workrooms are provided for the staff. The size, needs and financial resources of the Jewish community determine the size of the synagogue buildings.

sanctuary. The room where worship services are held. It is the heart of the synagogue and is beautifully furnished.

Besides the ark and the bimah, there are benches or chairs (without kneelers) for the congregation. The windows are usually stained glass, depicting such religious symbols as the Star of David, shofar, menorah, and tables of the law. Pictures of people may not be used in the sanctuary. On the bimah are a seven-branched menorah, lecterns, and chairs for the rabbi, cantor, officers, or important guests.

ark. A large cabinet-like structure that houses the Torah, usually built into the east wall of the sanctuary so that the congregation will face Jerusalem when attending services. Wherever the ark is, the congregation faces it. The ark has two doors, often richly carved. Sometimes, the ark has a beautiful curtain hanging in front of it.

bimah. The raised platform from which the Torah is read. The bimah is usually at the front of the sanctuary. In some sanctuaries, the bimah is in the center of the room and a railing surrounds it.

eternal flame. The lamp that hangs before the ark. It is lit as long as there is a Torah in the ark. In modern sanctuaries, an electric light may be used, though Orthodox congregations and some others may still use candles or oil. The light reminds the people that they are in the presence of God's word. The Roman Catholic Church has kept this custom of a lighted candle before the tabernacle (another word for ark) to remind the people that they are in the presence of God—the Blessed Sacrament.

menorah. The seven-branched candelabrum found in the sanctuary and lit for all services. In Exodus 25:31–40, we find specific directions given by God for making the menorah. It is displayed only on "holy ground." Since the first century this menorah has been a symbol of Judaism. It is also the symbol of the State of Israel.

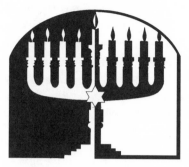

menorah

The Hanukkah menorah has eight candle holders, to commemorate the eight days of the holiday. A ninth candle, called the *shamash,* is used to light the eight candles as directed for the Hanukkah festival. This candelabrum is found in Jewish homes (Hanukkah is a home festival) as well as in the sanctuary during the days of the festival.

The Talmud (meaning "study"). Simply stated, the Talmud forms the core of the record of arguments, discussions, sayings, and writings of the biblical scholars as they interpreted the laws of the Torah to help the Jewish people observe the Torah in changing circumstances and to cope with life in foreign lands. The Talmud is the greatest literary achievement of the Jewish people and the most authoritative source on Judaism.

Torah. The first five books of the Bible: Genesis, Exodus, Leviticus, Numbers, and Deuteronomy. They are hand-printed in Hebrew by a scribe on a parchment scroll. Each end of the scroll is attached to a wooden pole or stave and then wound on the poles. Around the scroll is a band of cloth to prevent it from unwinding when not in use. Since it is the most precious possession of the Jews, the Torah is lovingly decorated. A mantle of rich cloth with ornate stitching covers it. A metal shield and the pointer used in reading the scroll are hung from the poles. Crowns are placed over the tops of the poles. Some crowns have little bells attached that tinkle when the Torah is moved. Because the script on the parchment could be damaged if a reader placed a hand on it while reading, a pointer (yad) is used. The Torah is "undressed" when brought to the reading table and then "dressed" after the completion of the reading(s).

yad (yod). The pointer used when reading the Torah. It can be very ornate and made of wood, precious metal, or ivory. There is a small hand with its index finger extended at the end of the pointer. Using it protects the precious parchment.

yarmulke. The Yiddish word for the head covering worn by men during morning prayer. In Hebrew it is called *kippah,* in English skullcap. No particular directions are given for the material, color, or style for the head covering. Reform and Reconstructionist Jews need not wear the yarmulke. Conservative Jews wear it for prayer. Orthodox Jews wear a head covering at all times. Today, many Jews wear the yarmulke in public, proudly proclaiming their Jewishness. Covering the head is an expression of humility before God.

Chapter 3

The Jewish Community Today*

While Jews consider themselves one people in fate and faith, they are divided into different groups or branches of religious practice, with variations in the synagogue service, the prayer book used, and observances in daily life. The three major branches of religious Judaism are Orthodox, Conservative and Reform Judaism. A numerically smaller branch, Reconstructionism, also plays a role in Jewish religious life today.

Orthodox Jews believe that a second complete law was revealed to Moses at Mt. Sinai along with the Ten Commandments and that it was passed from generation to generation by oral tradition without being written down for many centuries. This law, called the *halachah* (the "way" or the law) governs the daily life of Orthodox Jews—not only religious practice, but also every aspect of living: family behavior, business ethics, and issues of justice and charity. It is studied seriously and continuously as a source of moral instruction and religious inspiration. Orthodox Jews, for example, eat rabbinically approved (kosher) food, do not mix meat and

*Special thanks and acknowledgments are made for the contributions of Judith Banki, who wrote the text of Chapter 3, which was then reviewed and accepted by the author of the book, Anna Marie Erst.

dairy products at the meal, and will generally not ride in cars or do any manner of work or business on the Sabbath. Men wear a yarmulke (skullcap) in synagogue or at home during prayer or meals, since a head covering is considered a constant reminder that God is above all human activity. Orthodox synagogues usually have separate seating for men and women.

Reform Judaism, sometimes called Liberal or Progressive Judaism, originally distinguished between the ritual and the ethical teachings of the halachah, retaining the moral and ethical teachings but discarding many of the ritualistic rules. In recent years, however, Reform Judaism has reclaimed some of the ritualistic practice. There is a wide variation of practice among the Reform Jews, at home and in the synagogue. However, families generally sit together at services.

Conservative Judaism tries to maintain a middle path between the Reform and Orthodox positions. It upholds the authority of the halachah, but also acknowledges the need for change. Most Conservative synagogues have mixed seating, but some still maintain separate sections for men and for women.

Reconstructionism views Judaism as an evolving religious civilization rather than a set of religious beliefs. It therefore places great emphasis on learning Jewish history and the Hebrew language.

A special group within the Orthodox tradition, the *Hasidim,* have attracted much attention because of their rapid growth and a strong public presence. The Hasidim began in Eastern Europe, partly as a reaction against traditional Orthodoxy. They stressed joy and spontaneity in worship, dancing, singing, and mysticism as well as scholarship. Hasidic Jews claimed great powers for their rabbis, and a number of charming stories about the miraculous accomplishments of Hasidic leaders are now part of Jewish literature. There are several distinctive groups of Hasidim, generally named for their leader or their place of origin, and these groups wear distinctive garb.

There are some Jews who are not religiously observant but who live out a Jewish identification through giving to charity or joining Jewish communal or civic organizations that work for a better world. They affirm themselves as Jews and are so considered by other Jews.

Despite variations in religious practice, most Jews would agree on the central meaning of the major holidays. The Sabbath is set aside as a day of rest, a day free from the pressures of everyday life, a day for study, prayer, relaxed enjoyment, and the pleasures of family and companionship. In fact, the Sabbath is considered a foretaste of the perfected world of messianic times. The ten days called the High Holy Days or the Days of Awe, which link the Jewish New Year to the Day of Atonement *(Yom Kippur),* are a time for personal reflection and renewal, a time for Jews to make amends and to become reconciled with one another and with God.

In addition to variations in religious practice, Jews also reflect an enormous range of ethnic and national backgrounds. These backgrounds derive from very ancient times. When Jerusalem was destroyed in 586 B.C.E. (B.C.) by the Babylonian king Nebuchadnezzar, the Jews were deported to Babylon. The Persian king Cyrus, who conquered Babylonia some years later, allowed the Jews to return to Israel and rebuild their Temple. Jews who trace their ethnic origins to northern and eastern Europe *(Ashkenazim)* are the descendants of those who returned after the Babylonian exile and later spread throughout the Roman Empire, establishing settlements in Europe. Jews who trace their ethnic origins to Spain and Portugal *(Sephardim)* are the descendants of Jews who settled in the Mediterranean countries and the Middle East after their expulsion from Spain and Portugal. Some joined Jews who had stayed in Babylon, a community that was a major center of Jewish life and scholarship for more than one thousand years. Most Jews today trace their family histories back to the world of Christian Europe or the world of Muslim Spain, North Africa, and the Middle East. However, the first group of Jews who came to America did not come from these areas; they came from Brazil, arriving in 1654.

Since the creation of the State of Israel in 1948 as a homeland for persecuted Jews from every part of the world, historic Jewish communities from Ethiopia, India, Iran, Iraq, Egypt, and Morocco, along with the remnants who survived the Nazi holocaust in Europe, have been absorbed into the young nation.

HEROES AND HEROINES

Jews do not have saints. The Jewish people have had many martyrs, who willingly accepted death rather than deny or renounce Judaism. They are honored and remembered, but they are not called saints. Perhaps the closest thing to saints in the Jewish religion are the rabbis and sages who molded Judaism from a religion of animal sacrifice administered by a hereditary priesthood to a religion of study, prayer and good deeds, and helped it to survive after the destruction of the Temple in Jerusalem.

However, Jewish history does celebrate heroes and heroines. Some are biblical characters, like Judith; some, like Hillel, are sages and scholars who helped shape Jewish law; some are great scientists who also were great humanitarians, like Albert Einstein; and some, like Golda Meir, are communal leaders who dedicated their lives to the State of Israel.

Judith

The story of Judith is told in the Apocryphal book named for her, written during the Second Temple period. She was a pious and patriotic woman who saved her town of Bethulia from being destroyed by the armies of Nebuchadnezzar, king of Assyria. The advancing armies threatened to cut off the water supply. Judith dared to visit the commander, Holofernes, beguiled him with her beauty and charm, then killed him, saving the town.

Hillel

Hillel was a rabbinical authority and Pharisaic leader during the time of King Herod. Thus, he lived around the time of Jesus. He came to Jerusalem from Babylonia to perfect himself in biblical studies and tradition, founded an academy for the study of the law, the School of Hillel, and became the highest authority among the Pharisees and Scribes. He was known for his modesty, patience, and leniency. One legend holds that Hillel was asked by a potential convert to sum up the Jewish law while the man stood on one foot. Hillel replied, "What is hateful to you, do not do unto your fellow man. This is the whole law; all the rest is commentary. Go and learn it."

Rabbi Hillel and others like him, who studied and searched the Torah for its meaning for everyday life, were among the founders of the *Talmud*—a remarkable literary work that was compiled over a period of eight hundred years. The Talmud contains the teachings, discussions, agreements, and disagreements of Jewish scholars and rabbis over many years. It is a kind of textbook for Jewish living that covers every aspect of Jewish life. It provides instruction in such areas as agriculture, the celebration of festivals and feasts, marriage and divorce, and civil and criminal law. It also includes ethical teachings, history, and philosophy. The rules and regulations are tied to the Bible and are held by Orthodox Judaism to be as authoritative as the Bible itself.

Maimonides

Maimonides (Rabbi Moses ben Maimon) was the most famous Jewish figure in the post-talmudic period and one of the greatest religious thinkers of all time. A rabbinic authority, codifier of the law, philosopher and skilled doctor who served as physician to the sultan of Egypt, he was born in Córdoba, Spain, to a scholarly family in 1135. When Córdoba fell to a more militant and less tolerant Muslim group, the Almohads, who started persecuting Jews, his family left Spain and after much wandering, settled in Cairo, Egypt. Supported for years by his brother, he was able to devote himself to study, writing, and correspondence with Jewish religious leaders and scholars in other parts of the world. When his beloved brother drowned, he studied medicine to support his own and his brother's families, and because of his skill and reputation, became the sultan's physician. But he continued to study and to write, and he authored two monumental works of Jewish scholarship that are still studied today. He set himself the task of classifying by subject matter the entire talmudic and post-talmudic literature in a systematic manner that had never been attempted before—a task requiring, in his own words, "a broad mind, a wise soul, and considerable study."

Albert Einstein

This Nobel Prize–winning physicist and mathematician was a respected and beloved figure for Jews. His theory of relativity changed the way scientists understood the universe, and it was on the basis of a letter by Einstein to U.S. president Franklin Delano Roosevelt that the United States undertook a project to develop the first atomic bomb.

This remarkably creative thinker was born in Germany in 1879, but his family left when he was a teenager. He did not return until his scientific discoveries had made him world famous and he was offered a professorship at the University of Berlin. Even there he encountered anti-Semitism. He was not in Germany when Hitler came to power in 1933, and he never returned.

Einstein espoused pacifism until World War II, when he became convinced that only military might could defeat

Hitler. He also espoused Zionism—the conviction that the Jewish people must have a homeland of their own—and he helped establish the Hebrew University in Jerusalem in 1925—almost a quarter of a century before Israel became an independent nation. He was invited to be the first president of Israel but declined that honor.

Einstein did not practice traditional religion, but he believed in an orderly and logical universe. "God does not play dice with the universe" was one of his most famous statements. He was also a moral and compassionate human being who cared deeply about the world his discoveries changed forever.

Golda Meir

Golda Meir was a founder and the fourth prime minister of the State of Israel. A strong and courageous woman, she was born in Kiev, Russia, in 1898 and emigrated to the United States in 1906, settling in Milwaukee, Wisconsin. Childhood memories of Russian pogroms—massacres of Jews—helped form her as a Zionist. In 1921 she and her husband settled in Palestine, where she became associated with the Labor movement and proved to be an effective spokesperson for her movement and her people. On the eve of Israel's independence, she undertook a dangerous journey to meet with King Abdullah, then king of Jordan, urging him not to join the attack on the newborn Jewish State.

She served her country in many capacities. As minister to Russia, she defended the right of Russian Jews to leave the Soviet Union. As minister of labor (1949-1956), she initiated large-scale housing for new immigrants to Israel. As foreign minister, she extended financial and technical help to newly emerging African nations. In 1969 she was elected fourth prime minister of the State of Israel—the only woman to hold that position. When she died in 1978, it was discovered that she had had leukemia for twelve years.

Chapter 4

The Jewish Life Cycle

Jews and Christians alike believe that they have a special relationship to God. Both groups of believers, therefore, have traditions and ritual celebrations that remind them of this relationship and of God's goodness and holiness. Besides the holy days and festivals celebrated throughout the year, special ceremonies mark the major events in life: birth, coming of age, marriage, and death.

BIRTH

In Jewish tradition, a child born to a Jewish mother is Jewish. No rite, such as baptism, is required to make the child Jewish. But the birth of a child is an occasion of great joy and is marked in special ways.

Birth of a Boy

On the eighth day after his birth, a male child is circumcised and given his name, formally welcoming him into the covenant between God and Israel. *"Generation after generation, every male child shall be circumcised when he is eight days old"* (Gn 17:11–12).

The ceremony may take place in the home, in the synagogue, or in the hospital. A *mohel,* trained for the task, performs the circumcision, which is accompanied by prayers and blessings for the infant. The prayer naming the infant is: *"Our God and the God of our parents preserve this child _____ to manhood. Even as he has entered into the covenant, so may he enter into the study of the Torah, into the wedding canopy, and into a life of good deeds."* The ceremony is followed by a joyous celebration.

Birth of a Girl

On the Sabbath after the birth of a baby girl, her father is called up to read from the Torah. The prayer following the reading in which the child's name is announced is: *"He Who blest our fathers Abraham, Isaac, Moses and Aaron, David and Solomon, may He bless the mother _____ and her newborn daughter, whose name in Israel shall be _____. May her parents raise her for the marriage canopy and for a life of good deeds."* A festive celebration follows in the home in honor of the baby girl.

In recent years, some Jewish women have created new rituals for the birth of a girl to affirm the equal value of daughters and sons.

COMING OF AGE

Judaism does not require a rabbi for public worship. Any man or woman may lead the congregation in prayer in most congregations, though in Orthodox congregations this privilege is limited to men. The age at which a Jewish child is considered old enough to take on the responsibility of adulthood, to obey God's commandments, to fulfill religious obligations, and to lead the congregation in prayer is thirteen. This age was determined at a time when people matured earlier, married younger, and had shorter life expectancies.

Bar/Bat Mitzvah

The ritual ceremony of *bar mitzvah* (son of the command-ment) as we know it today dates back to the Middle Ages for boys. For girls, it is of recent origin. Because women were expected to be homemakers and mothers, their religious responsibilities were less exacting than those of the men. A simple ceremony celebrated in the home marked the coming of age for girls. Gradually, as equality of men and women was affirmed by liberal Jews, the ceremony of *bat mitzvah* (daughter of the commandment) was accepted and per-formed in the synagogue. The ceremony is the same for boys and girls.

A year of intense study precedes the bar/bat mitzvah cere-mony. The child studies Judaism in general, the Hebrew lan-guage, and the Torah portion to be read by him or her on the day of the ceremony. The entire congregation witnesses the child's coming of age and prays that he or she will be a faith-ful Jew. The child is *"called up to the Torah,"* where he or she chants the blessings and the day's section of the Torah and/or the Prophets in Hebrew. Usually the rabbi and the cantor stand on either side of the child in a gesture of welcome and support. After the blessing that concludes the reading(s), the rabbi blesses the child.

Frequently, following the ceremony but before the congrega-tion leaves the sanctuary, the father and mother and siblings (if there are any) join the child on the *bimah* (a raised platform from which the Torah is read) and tell of their joy and their love for the child. They pray for the child—very affirming actions. A reception or festive dinner follows, and the child receives con-gratulations and gifts from relatives and friends.

Confirmation

In the Reform movement, which began in Germany in the nineteenth century, a desire to improve the position of women in the synagogue brought about several changes. Family seating was introduced. Religious education for girls was required. Bar mitzvah was discontinued in favor of a new ceremony, confirmation, for both boys and girls. Confirmation became so popular that even some Conservative and Orthodox congregations adopted it.

However, bar mitzvah had been so traditional that it was missed by many. It was reintroduced, and the bat mitzvah for girls was added. Some congregations have continued the confirmation ceremony, but it is celebrated when boys and girls are about sixteen years old. The added years of study in preparation for confirmation enable the youths to gain a deeper insight into their faith and give them the opportunity to rededicate themselves to the promises made at the time of their bar/bat mitzvah.

Marriage

The importance of the family has always been central to Judaism. God's command to Adam and Eve to "be fruitful and multiply and fill the earth and make it yours" (Gn 1:28), according to Judaism, imposed upon men and women the obligation to marry and have children.

In ancient times, polygamy (marriage to more than one wife) was a common practice and was lawful even among the ancient Israelites. The patriarch Jacob was married to both Leah and her sister Rachel. The practice of polygamy is still found among the Bedouin peoples—wandering tribes. However, as Judaism evolved, its ideal of marriage became and remains monogamous: one husband, one wife. Intermarriage, marriage with a non-Jew, was and is frowned upon for several reasons. Children are Jewish only if born of a Jewish mother. Also, since the home is more important than the synagogue as a source of Jewish life, it is important that both parents help create a Jewish home. As in other religions, Jews hope marriage ties will last, but divorce is permitted and is regulated by Jewish law. The religious divorce, *get* in Hebrew, is granted by the husband to his wife. Without the get a wife may not remarry.

The marriage ceremony itself may differ in details according to the wishes and traditions of the bride and the bridegroom or of their parents. Three terms used in the ceremony may need clarification: *huppah*—the marriage canopy supported by four poles under which the bride and bridegroom stand during the ceremony and which represents the new home they will begin (the spelling of huppah may vary); **ring**—the bridegroom must prove before two witnesses that it is his and, therefore, his to freely give to his bride; and *ketubah*—the marriage contract, a legal document, stating that the bridegroom will care for his bride and will arrange for her support should he die before her or should they ever divorce. The ketubah was a beautifully hand-printed document in former times. Now it is often commercially printed, but it still is more or less ornate. Both the bride and bridegroom sign the ketubah before the marriage ceremony.

The bride and bridegroom may fast on their wedding day until the wedding. It is a private fast, a cleansing before beginning their new life together. The wedding ceremony may take place in the synagogue, the home, in a hotel, or wherever. The contemporary ceremony includes the betrothal and the wedding, which were two distinct ceremonies in earlier times, sometimes a year apart.

In traditional ceremonies, the bridegroom approaches his bride and covers her face with a veil. This action is said to date back to Jacob. At that time the bride's attendants covered her face before she was brought to join her bridegroom under the huppah. After the ceremony at Jacob's wedding, he discovered that he had been married to Leah instead of his beloved Rachel. He had to work another seven years for his Uncle Laban in order to win Rachel. Laban had feared that Leah would never be married if he allowed Rachel, his younger daughter, to marry first. From that time on, it is said, the bridegroom covered the bride's face. Jacob was lucky that in his time a man might have more than one wife.

The wedding ceremony begins when the bridegroom is led to the huppah by his male companions. His bride is then brought to him, and their parents join them under the huppah. The rabbi recites the betrothal blessing over a glass of wine, and the parents hand the glass to the bride and bridegroom, who sip from it. Then the bridegroom places the ring on the bride's finger, saying: "Behold, thou art consecrated to me by this ring according to the law of Moses and of Israel." In some congregations the bride gives her husband a ring as well, saying: "Be thou consecrated to me."

The rabbi then reads the ketubah and hands it to the bridegroom, who gives it to the bride. It is hers to keep. The rabbi recites the seven marriage blessings. The final blessing is:

> Blessed art Thou, O Lord our God, King of the Universe, Who created joy and gladness, bridegroom and bride, mirth, song, dancing, and jubilation, love and harmony, peace and fellowship. O Lord our God, may there soon be heard in the cities of Judah and the streets of Jerusalem the sound of joy and gladness, the voice of the groom and the bride, the jubilant voices of bridegrooms from their canopies and of youths from their feasts of song. Blessed art Thou, O Lord, Who causes the bridegroom to rejoice with the bride.

After the blessings the couple drink a second glass of wine. The bridegroom then crushes the glass from which he and his bride drank. This gesture recalls the destruction of the Temple in Jerusalem. According to some, it is a reminder to the couple that life does have its sorrows and difficulties, which they will share; according to others, it is a reminder that the joy of the wedding celebration should avoid "wild revelry."

After the ceremony, the bride and bridegroom spend a few

minutes alone. Then they rejoin their guests and enter into the wedding festivities.

DEATH AND MOURNING

Since the time of death is known only to God, we must always be prepared for it. Observant Jews who know that they are dying do what other religious people who believe in a loving, merciful God do. They praise God for his goodness, thank him for the gift of life, and ask his forgiveness for their shortcomings. They commend their loved ones to God's care and ask for a share in the world to come. The *Shema*—"Hear, O Israel, the Lord our God, the Lord is One"—is often the final prayer of a Jewish person.

When the members of the immediate family of a dead person hear of the death, they tear one of their garments or pin a piece of torn cloth to their clothing. Father, mother, sister, brother, son, daughter, and spouse are considered immediate family.

The body of the dead person is never left alone and is treated with respect. In former times, each congregation or group of congregations had a burial society that took care of the deceased. It was considered a great privilege to be a member of such a society. Perhaps the most important of good deeds was the preparation of the body for burial, because the deceased was unable to repay the good deed. The body was washed carefully, covered with a white shroud, and placed in a plain, wooden coffin. All was very simple. Today, undertakers perform this service. The deceased is dressed in a shroud or in his or her own clothes and placed in an ordinary coffin. The body of a man may be wrapped in his prayer shawl. A small packet of soil from Israel is sometimes placed behind the neck of the deceased. This custom probably comes from a tradition that on the day when the dead will arise, those buried in Israel will be the first to rise from the dead. The hope is that those who have a packet of soil from Israel buried with them will be included with those who were actually buried in Israel.

Burial

Burial is mandated for traditional Jews and takes place on the day of death or the following day, if possible. Jews do not practice embalming, so prompt burial is essential. The coffin is closed. Among many Jews it is considered an intrusion and even disrespectful to gaze upon a dead person. However, the immediate family may view the body before the coffin is closed. It is customary to make a donation in the name of the deceased to some charity or deserving cause rather than to send flowers.

The funeral service includes prayers, psalms, and tributes to the deceased by family members, friends, and colleagues. After the concluding prayer, relatives and friends join the family to escort the deceased to the cemetery. A brief ceremony takes place at the grave. The coffin is lowered into the grave and all present, beginning with the members of the immediate family, in turn, throw three shovelsful of dirt upon the coffin. This action helps to make the death a reality.

Mourning

A formal period of mourning begins in the home after the burial. As the mourners leave the cemetery, friends may speak words of sympathy to the family. The traditional words are: "May the Lord comfort you among the mourners in Zion and Jerusalem." Those who attended the funeral or burial will wash their hands before entering their home or the home of the deceased. This is an ancient act of purification after having had contact with the dead. At the entrance to the home of the deceased, a basin of water and some towels are placed upon a table for this purpose.

Sitting Shiv'a

For seven days following the burial, the members of the immediate family refrain from leaving the home (except for the Sabbath). In some homes the mirrors are covered as a gesture of turning away from human vanity. No work is done by family members. Their needs are attended to by neighbors, who bring in food, care for the little children, if there are any, and see to it that there is a *minyan* (ten Jews who have made their bar/bat mitzvah) to say the prayers in the home. A candle is kept burning in memory of the deceased. These seven days of mourning are known as "sitting shiv'a." *Shiv'a* is the Hebrew word for seven.

From the eighth day to the thirtieth day, mourners still forgo festivities. The *Kaddish,* the mourner's prayer, which does not mention death but praises God and asks for his peace for all, is said by a member of the immediate family. If the deceased is a parent, the Kaddish is continued for eleven months. After that, the mourning period is over.

Yahrzeit

On the anniversary of the person's death, the Kaddish is said at the synagogue by a member of the family or some designated person, and a candle is lit in memory of the deceased. This anniversary rite, repeated yearly, is known as *Yahrzeit,* a German word meaning "year time."

General Notes

Orthodox and most Conservative Jews always bury their dead. They look upon cremation as a mutilation of the body that prevents the normal disintegration of the body. It voids the statement in Genesis:

"Remember, you are dust and to dust you will return" (Gn 3:19). Reform and Reconstructionist Jews accept cremation if it is the choice of the deceased or of the family. For some Jews, cremation reminds them of the horrors of the holocaust. For many, the closure of the grave is desirable.

Usually one does not see flowers on the graves in Jewish cemeteries. Flowers are considered an expression of joy, and cemeteries are places of somber reflection. Visitors leave small stones on the tombstone or grave as a sign of their visit. Tombstones, markers, or plaques mark the graves, giving the name of the deceased, date of birth and death, etc. Frequently, both Hebrew and the local language appear on the marker.

Though death marks the end of earthly life, it also opens the door to eternal life. Judaism has no single idea about an afterlife. There is belief that the departed soul of a good person is gathered to God. For those of us who believe in God as our loving Father, eternal rest and happiness with God is what we desire for our loved ones when death claims them—and what we hope for when our own earthly life comes to an end.

> He will swallow up death forever,
> And the Lord will wipe away
> Tears from all faces,
> And the reproach of His people He will remove
> From all the earth;
> For the Lord has spoken. (Is 25:8)

candle and Tables of the Law

Chapter 5

The Jewish Festivals

An excellent way to help us understand and appreciate the beliefs and traditions of our Jewish neighbors is to learn about some of their festivals. A brief explanation is given below of the principal feasts. As each festival occurs, you might share the meaning and manner of the festival's celebration with your classmates. You could become a bridge-builder between the Jewish people and their non-Jewish neighbors. You would be helping to build God's kingdom on earth.

There is a distinction between our holy days and the Jewish festivals. Most of our Christian holy days celebrate the life, death, and resurrection of Jesus Christ. Most of the Jewish festivals recall events related to the interaction between God and the whole Jewish people. Except for the high holy days, which are of a purely spiritual nature, the festivals recount historic episodes that the Jews experienced as a community, such as the Exodus (Passover), the giving of the Torah at Sinai (Shavuot), and the years of wandering in the desert (Sukkot). Thus, the Jewish children learn their people's history through celebrating the festivals.

The Jewish calendar is a lunar calendar, based on the phases of the moon. The Jewish year has 353, 354, or 355 days, divided into twelve months. A thirteenth month is added in leap years. The Jewish year begins in September or October (see the calendar on the following page). Creation is dated at 3761 B.C.E. (before the Christian era) and there is no division between B.C.E. and C.E. (Christian era) or B.C. and A.D. The year 1996 is the Jewish year 5757. To determine the Jewish year, just add the current year to 3761: 1996 + 3761 = 5757.

There are three classifications of Jewish festivals:

1. **The High Holy Days:** From Rosh Hashanah to and including Yom Kippur. The period through Yom Kippur is known as the **Ten Days of Penitence,** during which each person examines his or her conscience and behavior and prays for forgiveness of sins and for a good year.

2. **The Pilgrimage Festivals:** Passover, Shavuot, and Sukkot. These are the days on which the Jews were required to make a pilgrimage to the Temple in Jerusalem and bring an offering to God. Each has a threefold significance: agricultural, historical, and spiritual.

3. **The Lesser or Minor Festivals:** The best known are Hanukkah, Purim, Lag b'Omer, Tu b'Shevat and, in our times, Israel Independence Day.

The dates of the festivals are movable. The dates may be obtained from a synagogue, a rabbi, a Jewish calendar, or a Jewish art shop. Some ordinary calendars note them, too.

The observance of Jewish festivals always begins at sunset the day before the actual date and ends at sunset on the day itself. This is so because the Torah states that God considered the evening as the beginning of the day: *"Evening passed and morning came, that was the first day"* (Gn 1:15).

It is very important that we Catholics—and all Christians— make every effort to understand and respect our Jewish neighbors. They have suffered much through the centuries at the hands of misguided Christians. From this stem the demeaning stereotypes and prejudices society has had—and to some extent still has—about the Jews.

Calendar for the Jewish Festivals

Fall	**TISHRE** (tish REE) (Celebrated as New Year) SEPT.-OCT.	**HESHVAN** (hesh VONN) (Marheshvan) OCT.-NOV.	**KISLEV** (kis LEV) NOV.-DEC.
Winter	**TEVET** (tay VET) DEC.-JAN.	**SHEVAT** (shuh VOTT) JAN.-FEB.	**ADAR** (ad DARR) Occurs twice in leap year FEB.-MAR.
Spring	**NISAN** (nee SANN) 1st month of year in ancient times MAR.-APR.	**IYAR** (ee YARR) APR.-MAY	**SIVAN** (see VONN) MAY-JUNE
Summer	**TAMMUZ** (tah MOOZ) JUNE-JULY	**AV** (av) JULY-AUG.	**ELUL** (el LOOL) AUG.-SEPT.

THE SABBATH DAY

"Remember the Sabbath day, to keep it holy. Six days shall you labor and do your work, but the seventh day is a Sabbath to the Lord your God. In it you shall not do any work." (Ex 20:8-10)

The most important, most sacred and joyous day for the Jewish people is the Sabbath. This seventh day of the week is a sign of the covenant between God and his people. God himself commanded it to be observed as a special day of prayer and rest, a day devoted to God and one's family. It is one of the Ten Commandments given to Moses on Mt. Sinai.

Jews of different religious orientations observe the Sabbath in different ways. For example, Orthodox Jews will not drive cars or use public transportation. They will walk to the synagogue. Conservative and Reform Jews generally interpret Sabbath regulations more liberally. But for all Jews, the Sabbath is meant to be a day of spiritual renewal and physical relaxation, a time of turning away from worldly cares and financial concerns. In Jewish tradition, the Sabbath is regarded as a foretaste of the world to come, a time of peace and harmony.

There is not the same obligation for the Jewish people to attend the Sabbath services in the synagogue as there is for Roman Catholics to attend mass on Sunday or Saturday evening. The Jewish people are urged to attend the synagogue services on the Sabbath. Formerly only the men were expected to attend. The women were excused since they had to have all in readiness in the home for the celebration of the Sabbath. If they did attend they were seated in a balcony or in a room next to the sanctuary with large openings in the wall to enable them to follow the services.

Today, practicing Jews attend as a family. The Orthodox and some Conservative Jews still maintain a special section for women, but in all other congregations the people sit wherever they wish. Benches or chairs are provided for the members of the congregation. Kneelers are not needed, as people pray seated or standing during the service. In Orthodox or Conservative synagogues a box of yarmulkes is placed at the entrance of the sanctuary for males older than thirteen who forgot theirs or are visiting. All males are required to wear a yarmulke for the service.

Entering the sanctuary one finds the rabbi and cantor (in all but Orthodox and some Conservative congregations these may be male or female) on the bimah. The officers of the congregation and important guests may also be seated on the bimah. The members of the congregation have prayer books to enable them to follow the service and, at times, to participate. Some parts of the service may be recited or sung in Hebrew. The rabbi or cantor takes care of these. The rabbi indicates when the congregation is to stand or sit and announces the page of the service as it progresses, as not all of the prayers are said at any one service.

The service itself consists of prayers of praise, gratitude, and petition, readings, songs, and short meditations. When it is time for the readings, the rabbi opens the ark and takes out the Torah, giving it to the reader of the day, who brings it to the table or lectern. Blessings are recited before the readings. Following the readings from the Torah, a portion from the Prophets is read. Blessings are again recited, and the Torah is returned to the ark. The rabbi then gives a sermon, usually relating the teachings from the readings to daily life, much like the priest's or minister's homily.

The service is concluded by the recitation of the Kaddish, which is sometimes referred to as the mourners prayer but is really a prayer of praise to God and of gratitude for the gift of memory that enables us to remember those who have gone before us and "links generation to generation."

Because the handling of money is forbidden on the Sabbath and other major holidays, no collections are taken up at synagogue services. The obligation to support the Jewish community is fulfilled by contributions to the synagogue at other times. Other charitable institutions are supported in similar ways.

Observance of the Sabbath is a great gift to us from Judaism. Without the weekly day of rest, we would have no respite from work, no special time for praising God together, no time to enjoy our family, no weekend.

In preparation for the Sabbath, the home is thoroughly cleaned, the dinner table is covered with a fresh tablecloth, the best dishes and tableware and the Sabbath candles are set out. The best food is kept for the Sabbath. A pitcher of sweet wine, the Kiddush cup and two loaves of freshly baked bread (usually braided) complete the table preparation. The two loaves of bread remind those present of the double portion of manna collected on the day before the Sabbath when their ancestors journeyed in the desert.

Just before sundown, when all is in readiness, the family having donned their good clothes, the mother lights and blesses the candles, asking God's blessing on her family and home. The father then may praise his wife by quoting a passage from the Book of Proverbs or thank her in his own words for all she does for the family. Then he fills the Kiddish cup with wine and recites the ***Kiddush,*** a prayer of blessing that has been recited since ancient times:

> Blessed be Thou, O Lord our God, Creator of the fruit of the vine. Blessed be Thou, our God, Ruler of the world, who sanctified us by Thy commandments and wast pleased with us and hast given us for a heritage, in love and favor, the holy Sabbath, a memorial of the going forth from Egypt. Blessed be Thou, O Lord, who hallowest the Sabbath.

The cup of wine is passed to each person. All sip from it. Next, the father breaks the bread, saying: *"Praised art Thou, O Lord, our God, Ruler of the universe, who brings forth bread from the earth."*

A piece of the bread is given to each person. The father blesses his children. Laying his hands on their heads, he says: *"May the Lord bless you and keep you. May He send His light into your lives and deal graciously with you. May He look favorably upon you and grant you shalom, peace."* The Sabbath meal is then served. Songs may be sung or stories told during and/or after the meal to add to its joyousness.

The Sabbath day itself is spent in prayer, study, relaxation, and the companionship of family and friends. The day comes to a close after sunset (Saturday) with a ceremony known as **havdalah,** meaning "to set aside," for God set aside the Sabbath from all other days. A braided candle, called the havdalah candle, is lit, denoting the beginning of the week of work days. Lighting a fire of any kind is forbidden on the Sabbath: *"You shall kindle no fire in all your habitations on the Sabbath"* (Ex 35:3). The havdalah candle has two or more wicks because it is made with two rather thin candles, giving it a flat, wide appearance. It is braided because the blessings of the Sabbath should permeate the entire week. The Sabbath enters and departs in the warm glow of candlelight.

After the havdalah candle is lit, the Kiddush cup is filled with wine and blessed. The spice box, a perforated box containing precious spices, is then blessed and passed around for all to inhale the spices' perfume, recalling the sweetness of a Sabbath well spent.

The prayers and blessings as well as the order of the havdalah ceremony may differ from home to home. Some Reform Jews have eliminated it altogether. At the conclusion of the havdalah ceremony, the cup of wine is passed for each to sip from it, careful to leave a small amount in the cup. When all have had a sip, the leader takes the havdalah candle and extinguishes it by dipping it into the remnant of wine.

The peace and hope from a Sabbath well observed are reflected in a prayer from the synagogue service:

Strengthen the bonds of friendship and fellowship among the inhabitants of all lands. Plant virtue in every soul, and may the love of Thy Name hallow every home and heart. Praised be Thou, O Lord, Giver of Peace.

ROSH HASHANAH—THE JEWISH NEW YEAR

"May you be inscribed for a good year!"
This is the traditional greeting among Jews on Rosh

Hashanah. *Rosh Hashanah* means "first of the year." It is observed on the first day of Tishre (which comes in September or October). Most Orthodox and Conservative Jews observe two days; Reform Jews observe only the first day. It ushers in a period of ten days of penitence during which the Jewish people examine their lives, pray for forgiveness and ask God's blessing for the coming year. These are solemn days, not sad ones. But they are not the merrymaking days associated with the New Year celebrations of January 1.

In Numbers 29:1-2, we read: "On the first day of the seventh month you are to gather for worship and no work is to be done. On that day the shofar is to be blown."

shofar

The *shofar,* a ram's horn, was used in ancient times to call the people together. Its sound is sharp and piercing and special skill is needed to sound it. On Rosh Hashanah it is sounded during the morning service. Each time three short, abrupt blasts, a long wavering blast, and nine staccato blasts are blown. The sounding of the shofar reminds the people of:

— God's kingship—The shofar was sounded at the coronation of the kings of Israel.

- The giving of the Torah at Sinai—*"The sound of the shofar waxed louder and louder; Moses spoke and God answered him"* (Ex 19:19).

- God's judgment of his people—*"This day the world was created; this day all creatures of the universe stand in judgment before You, O God"* (Rosh Hashanah liturgy).

- The coming of the messianic age—*"On that day a great shofar shall be sounded"* (Is 27:13).

- The need to be ready to give one's life for one's faith. The story of Abraham and Isaac is read during the service.

Some of the customs connected with Rosh Hashanah are:

- A joyful dinner on the eve of the festival. The mother lights and blesses the candles. The father blesses the cup of holiday wine and shares it with those present. Pieces of apple dipped in honey are eaten, expressing the hope that the coming year will be one of sweetness.

- The father blesses his children, laying his hands on their heads and asking God to keep them true to their tradition and grant them a good year.

- The traditional greeting, "May you be inscribed for a good year!" is exchanged as people meet.

- Greeting cards are sent to relatives and friends.

(The days following Rosh Hashanah culminating in Yom Kippur may be likened to Lent, the period of penance for many Christians.)

In conclusion, let us join our Jewish neighbors in prayer from the evening service of Rosh Hashanah:

Bless our country that it may ever be a stronghold of peace, and its advocate in the council of nations. May contentment reign within its borders, health and happiness within its homes. Strengthen the bonds of friendship and fellowship among the inhabitants of our land. Plant virtue in every soul, and may the love of Thy Name hallow every home and every heart. Inscribe us in the book of life, and grant unto us a year of prosperity and joy. Praised be Thou, O Lord, Giver of peace. (New Union Prayer Book)

YOM KIPPUR—DAY OF ATONEMENT

The most solemn day in the Jewish year is Yom Kippur, the tenth day after Rosh Hashanah. It is a day of prayer and total fasting from sunset to sunset.

And it shall be a statute forever unto you: in the seventh month, on the tenth day of the month, you shall afflict your souls, and do no manner of work, you nor the stranger that lives among you. For on this day shall atonement be made to cleanse you. From all your sins shall you be clean before the Eternal One. It is a Sabbath of solemn rest unto you and you shall afflict your souls. It is a statute forever. (Lv 16:29-32)

Before the fast of Yom Kippur begins, the family enjoys a festive meal because the approaching fast, although solemn, is not a sad occasion and will bring upon them God's grace. As on Rosh Hashanah, the children are blessed. Once the fast begins, no food or drink is taken if at all possible, and the time is spent in prayer until the end of the closing ceremony. Even the children fast and pray at least for part of the day.

Prior to the day, many Jews make donations to charitable causes, a way of showing their sincerity in making amends for past failures. The obligation to give charity ranks very high in Jewish tradition.

The Yom Kippur fast is more than just a penance. It is a form of self-discipline, a means of concentrating on the spirit. It enables one to realize the plight of the poor, who are often hungry for many days, and, it is hoped, awakens compassion for them.

The best-known and best-loved part of the Yom Kippur service is the Kol Nidre prayer, which is chanted at the evening service. It has a beautiful, plaintive melody accompanying very moving words. *Kol Nidre* means "all vows." The prayer asks God to forgive the members of the congregation for any vows made to him that they have not been able to fulfill. It does not release one from promises made to others. Such promises must be settled between the parties themselves.

The theme that permeates not only Yom Kippur but all the ten days is that of reconciliation between people as a necessary prelude to reconciliation with God. The asking of forgiveness must be accompanied by some form of restitution and a resolution to do better in the future. The lesson of Yom Kippur is that the fast and prayer are acceptable to God only if they lead to good deeds.

A memorial service for the dead is held as part of the day's service. The memory of loved ones is recalled in such prayers as:

We remember all our beloved who have already reached the goal whither we are tending. We think of the days when they were with us, and we rejoice in the blessing of their companionship and affection. They are near us even now.

The mourner's Kaddish is recited to close the memorial service. The concluding portion of the Yom Kippur service extols God's glory and his great mercy. As sunset approaches, the end of the day of prayer and fasting is announced by a blast of the shofar.

Benediction

> *And now, at the close of this day's service, we implore Thee, O Lord our God: Let the year upon which we have entered be for us, for Israel and for all mankind: A year of salvation and comfort; A year of peace and contentment, of joy and of spiritual welfare; A year which finds the hearts of parents united with the hearts of their children; A year of Thy pardon and favor. May the Lord bless thy going out and thy coming in from this time forth and forever. Amen.*

Assured of God's love, in a spirit of joy the people return home.

SUKKOT—THE FESTIVAL OF TABERNACLES (HOSHANAH RABBA/SIMHATH TORAH)

On the 15th of Tishre, the Jewish community celebrates a most joyous festival: Sukkot (pronounced sue-coat). It comes just five days after Yom Kippur, and its celebration lasts for nine days. The first two and the last two days are full holidays, while the days in between are "half-holidays," that is, days on which special prayers are said, but adults may go to work and children to school. It is a harvest festival and one of the three pilgrimage festivals on which Jews were required to go to the Temple in Jerusalem to pray and to give gifts to God in thanksgiving for his goodness to them.

As well as being a harvest festival of thanksgiving, Sukkot has a historical significance. It commemorates the forty years the Jews wandered in the desert—where they lived in temporary shelters—on their way to the Promised Land after leaving Egypt. For this reason the festival is sometimes referred to as the Feast of Tabernacles or the Feast of Booths, tabernacles and booths being names for shelters.

To make the commemoration realistic, where possible, Jewish families erect a *sukkah* (booth, hut) outside their homes. All members of the family take part in building the sukkah. A fragile framework is made for its walls, and the roof is covered with branches and leaves, leaving an opening to the sky so one can contemplate heaven. The structure is colorfully decorated with fruits and vegetables. The fragile, temporary character of the sukkah serves as a reminder that material things are not lasting, that for salvation one must depend on God, who is eternal. The family gathers for meals in the sukkah during the festival days.

Today, because so many families live in apartment buildings and families are smaller, Jewish congregations often build a large sukkah next to the synagogue that can accommodate all its members. If a synagogue in your neighborhood has a sukkah, it would be well worthwhile to arrange to visit it.

During the services in the synagogue, the rabbi or cantor holds a *lulav* (a palm branch with a few sprigs of myrtle and willow) in one hand and a citron (a lemon-like fruit of the Holy Land) in the other. These he waves in all directions to signify that God is everywhere. Worshipers who have their own lulav and citron join in this waving. This custom may also be carried out during prayer in the family sukkah, especially if children are present.

Hoshanah Rabba

The seventh day of the festival is known as *Hoshanah Rabba*—the great hosannas—noting the end of the final judgment of persons that was begun on Rosh Hashanah. In most synagogues the members proceed around the synagogue seven times singing hosannas, prayers for salvation.

When the congregation assembles in the synagogue on the eighth day—a full festival day—a special prayer is said for rain so that good crops might be had in the coming year. This prayer is said even if torrential rain is falling at the time!

Simhath Torah

The ninth and final day of Sukkot is a very special day of rejoicing known as *Simhath Torah*. This day completes the reading of the Torah in the synagogue and begins its rereading. At the evening service, the Torah is held aloft and carried around the synagogue; the children follow, carrying banners and singing songs. Then, a section of Deuteronomy—the last book of the Torah—is read. In the morning, another such procession takes place. Then the final section of Deuteronomy is read, followed by the first chapter of Genesis.

During the service there is an air of great expectation among the children, for on this very special day even children may be called to the bimah to recite the blessings. In many Reform and Conservative congregations, little children who have been enrolled in religion classes for the first time are brought up to the open ark and there receive their first lesson from the Torah. They are given miniature Torahs and chocolates—a combination meant to show the sweetness of God's word.

The joyous celebration of Sukkot as a harvest festival thanking God for his goodness to us is like our American Thanksgiving. Many historians believe that the Pilgrims got their idea for the Thanksgiving feast from reading about Sukkot in the Bible.

HANUKKAH—THE FESTIVAL OF DEDICATION

In the month of December when Christians are celebrating the wondrous feast of Christmas, the Jews are celebrating one of their most joyous and best-loved holidays: Hanukkah. It occurs on the twenty-fifth of Kislev. Unlike Christmas, which is a major feast for Christians, Hanukkah is a minor festival in the Jewish calendar.

Perhaps you have noticed the eight-branched menorah (candelabrum) in the windows of Jewish homes or visible inside. Why an eight-branched menorah? Why eight days of celebration?

More than two thousand years ago, when the Syrian-Greek, Antiochus Epiphanes, ruled Judea, he prohibited the practice of Judaism under pain of death. He seized the Temple in Jerusalem and turned it into a place of pagan worship.

In Modin, Judea, Mattathias, a respected leader of the people, encouraged the Jews to revolt. He, his five sons, and many followers fled to the mountains. There Mattathias died, but one of his sons, Judah, organized an army and, after three years of struggle, managed to regain Jerusalem and its Temple.

Judah was given the name Maccabee, which means "hammer," because of his repeated attacks (hammer blows) on the Syrians in the struggle to regain Jerusalem.

The Jews then cleansed and purified the Temple and rededicated it to God. According to legend, the Jews found only one cruse (a jar or pot) of holy oil with the high priest's seal intact at the Temple—enough to keep the lamp called the eternal flame, which hung in front of the ark, lit for one day. Miraculously, the oil lasted for eight days, giving the priests time to prepare oil to keep the eternal flame alight without interruption. Judah Maccabee proclaimed an eight-day festival to be celebrated annually to commemorate the rededication of the Temple. The festival was called *Hanukkah,* which means "dedication."

Hanukkah is very much a children's festival—a time for fun, songs, games, and gift-giving. Though there are special prayers and the lighting of the menorah candles with the accompanying blessings in the synagogue daily, the home is the center of the celebration. Home activities include:

1. *The Hanukkah menorah* (which has eight candles plus a holder for the *shamash,* the candle used to light the others) *is lit.* One candle is lit the first evening, two the second, and so on until all eight are lit on the eighth day. Before lighting the candles, the following blessings are recited:

   "Praised are You, O Lord our God, King of the Universe, Who sanctified us with Your commandments and commanded us to kindle the Hanukkah light.

   "Praised are You, O Lord our God, King of the Universe, who performed wondrous deeds for our ancestors in ancient days at this season."

   On the first day is added:

   "Praised are You, O Lord our God, King of the Universe, Who kept us in life, sustained us, and enabled us to reach this season."

2. *Gifts are exchanged.* Traditionally, children receive a simple gift each day.

3. *Parties are given for relatives and friends.* A favorite treat at the parties are *latkes* (pancakes). These pancakes are made from one's favorite recipe—in eastern Europe potato pancakes are the favorite. The pancakes are fried in oil to recall the cruse of miraculous oil that burned for eight days. They are served with sour cream and/or applesauce.

4. *Games are played.* The most popular of Hanukkah games is dreidel. The *dreidel* is a top, usually four-sided, with a Hebrew letter on each side—the first letter in the four Hebrew words meaning "A great miracle happened there." In Israel, the statement is changed to "A great miracle happened here." This refers, again, to the cruse of oil that burned for eight days. Rules for the dreidel game are given on pp. 52–53.

5. *Charity* (tzedakah) *is collected for the poor.*

In postholocaust years, Hanukkah has become very important to adults as well as to children. Its theme of religious freedom has taken on a deeper meaning. It symbolizes the triumph of faith in God over force: *Not by might, nor by power, but by My Spirit, saith the Lord of Hosts.*

Hanukkah is a national holiday in Israel, where it is celebrated with pilgrimages and parades as well as with parties, songs, and games. It has a unique meaning for all Americans, too. It commemorates the first uprising in history for the sake of freedom of religion.

Hanukkah is often called the Festival of Lights. One of the prayers in the synagogue service is: *"Let the lights we kindle shine forth for the world. May they illumine our lives even as they fill us with gratitude that our faith has been saved from extinction time and time again."*

dreidels

The Dreidel Game

The dreidel game is most fun when not more than six players take part. All players have tokens or coins of the same value. Hanukkah *gelt*—gold foil-covered chocolate coins in small net bags—is popular. These are found around the time of the Hanukkah festival wherever candy is sold. All players contribute the agreed amount into the "pot" and then spin the dreidel in turn. When the dreidel stops spinning, if the uppermost Hebrew letter is

- *nun*   (**נ**)   the player gets nothing;
- *gimel* (**ג**)   the player takes the entire pot, and all must feed the pot again;
- *hey*   (**ה**)   the player takes half the pot—or one half plus one if the pot contains an even number of tokens;
- *shin* (**ש**)   the player adds to the pot.

These are the usual rules; they may vary. Songs may be sung during the play. The formation of the Hebrew letters and the spelling of Hebrew words may vary slightly, but they should be recognizable from the examples above.

PURIM—THE FESTIVAL OF LOTS

Masks, costumes, plays, dances, jollity—a carnival-like festival air permeates Purim, celebrated on the fourteenth day of Adar (February-March). It commemorates the delivery of the Jews in Persia from persecution and death in ancient times. The story is found in the book of Esther, named for the Jewish queen whose courage helped to save her people.

In the days of the Persian king Ahasuerus, there was an evil prime minister, Haman, whose anger was aroused by the refusal of Mordecai, a Jew, to bow before him. Haman decided that all the Jews in Persia should be killed. On a trumped-up charge, he managed to get the king to sign a decree ordering the massacre of the Jews. He threw lots (dice known as *purim*) to determine the date of the attack upon the Jews. The numbers on the lots were thirteen and twelve, which Haman took to mean the thirteenth day of the twelfth month (Adar). The festival received its name from this: Purim or the Festival of Lots.

Mordecai's niece Esther had become Ahasuerus' queen, and Mordecai convinced Esther to act to save her people. Because she risked death in approaching the king unless summoned, Esther and all the Jews fasted for three days.

Then Esther dressed herself in royal garb and approached the king. He received her, and Esther pleaded for the Jews. The king then ordered Haman hanged on the scaffold that had been prepared for Mordecai.

Since the order to attack the Jews could not be rescinded, Ahasuerus allowed the Jews to arm themselves in self-defense. When the thirteenth of Adar arrived, the Jews, being well prepared, were victorious. On the fourteenth they celebrated their victory.

As mentioned earlier, a carnival atmosphere permeates Purim. There are parties, plays, and dances. Children make masks and dress up in imaginative costumes, portraying in a playful manner the characters in this and in other biblical stories. More serious programs are given in many Hebrew schools and in synagogues. At parties, the traditional *hamantashen,* delicious three-cornered pastries with jam or poppy-seed filling, are served (recipe given on pp. 55–56). The three-cornered shape supposedly represents Haman's hat.

On the eve of Purim, the reading from the book of Esther in the synagogue is a merry occasion. The children are given *groggers* (noisemakers), and every time Haman's name is mentioned they stamp their feet, twirl the groggers, and make as much noise as possible. Some even write Haman's name on the soles of their shoes in chalk, rubbing it out as they stamp their feet.

The following morning, the reading of the book of Esther is concluded with prayers of thanksgiving that faith triumphed over hatred. One of the prayers from the synagogue service reads: *"Blessed is the Lord our God, Ruler of the*

Universe, Who performed wondrous deeds for our ancestors in the days of old, at this season."

Purim recalls the courage of Queen Esther, who stood up for her people at great personal risk. It also reminds us that though evil may seem all-powerful at times, it can be defeated if people of good faith work together.

Grant us, O Lord, the vision to see and the courage to do Your will. Imbue our hearts with the fidelity of Mordecai and the devotion of Esther, that we may never swerve from the path of duty and loyalty to our heritage. Endow us with patience and strength, with purity of heart and unity of purpose, that we may continue to proclaim Your law of love and truth to the people of the earth, until all have learned that they are one, the children of the Eternal God. Amen. (From the Purim service)

RECIPE FOR HAMANTASHEN

Dough:
4 cups all-purpose flour
1 cup sugar
3 teaspoons baking powder
1/2 teaspoon salt
3 large eggs, beaten
4 tablespoons orange juice
1 cup margarine or butter softened
  to room temperature

Filling:
3 ounces cream cheese,
  softened
2 teaspoons jam (any flavor)
1/4 cup chopped nuts

Cream the margarine or butter and the sugar together in a large bowl. Add the eggs and orange juice. Mix well.

In a separate bowl, mix the flour, baking powder, and salt. Add this to the sugar and egg mixture. Mix well with a large spoon. Refrigerate for about an hour.

Sprinkle flour on the rolling pin and the surface to be used for rolling out the dough. Roll the dough to $1/4$-inch thickness.

Using a glass, mug or cookie cutter about 3 inches in diameter, cut the dough in circles.

Mix the filling ingredients. Drop about $3/4$ teaspoon of filling in the center of each circle. Shape into triangles by bringing two sides up to the center of the circle and pinching the dough together.

Bring up the third side and pinch to the other two sides. Be sure that the dough is pinched securely at the ends; do not close the top completely, so the filling will show.

Preheat oven to 350 degrees. Place the cookies on greased cookie sheets about an inch apart. Bake for ten to twelve minutes until lightly browned.

PASSOVER (PESACH)

Passover, probably the most beloved of all the Jewish festivals, occurs on the fifteenth day of Nisan (March-April). In ancient times, the Jews were required to make a pilgrimage to the Temple in Jerusalem, bringing an offering to God. Mary and Joseph fulfilled this duty, as we know from the gospel story that Jesus, at the age of twelve, accompanied them on the pilgrimage.

The celebration of Passover is observed for eight days. Orthodox and Conservative Jews observe the first two and the last two days as full holidays; Reform Jews observe the first and last days. The days in between are half-holidays, that is, days on which special prayers and customs are observed, but adults may go to work and the children to school.

The central ceremony of the festival is the seder, which is both a meal and a worship service celebrated in the home on the eve of Passover. The entire family gathers around a festive dinner table for the occasion. Friends, neighbors, and even strangers who are unable to be in their own homes are invited to share in the festivities. The celebration centers around the story of the Exodus.

Those present are given copies of the haggadah, a book explaining the order of the ceremony. The Hebrew word for "order" is *seder,* and *haggadah* means "telling"—in this instance, the telling of the story of God's intervention in freeing his people from slavery in Egypt. This fulfills the biblical injunction: *"Thou shalt tell thy son in that day saying, 'It is because of that which the Lord did for me when I came forth out of Egypt'"* (Ex 13:8).

The youngest child opens the celebration by asking four questions, beginning with: "Why is this night different from all other nights?"

In answering, the father recalls how God freed His people, the Israelites, from slavery under the pharaoh. He tells the story as if it had happened to him personally, not just to his ancestors. In this way, each generation of Jews relives the emancipation experience as its own.

The prayers they say bless and thank God for his deliverance. Often, they link to the story of the past such contemporary freedom struggles as that of the Soviet Jews.

To emphasize the events of the Exodus story, special foods adorn a seder plate: three **matzohs,** wafers of unleavened bread that recall the haste with which the Jews had to bake their bread dough when leaving Egypt (Passover is sometimes called The Festival of Unleavened Bread because only matzohs are permitted during the eight days of celebration); **maror,** bitter herbs, a reminder of their slavery in Egypt; **haroseth,** a mixture of chopped apples, nuts, cinnamon, and wine symbolizing the mortar used by the Jewish slaves to hold bricks together when making pharaoh's buildings; **a shank bone,** a reminder of the sacrificial lamb; **a roasted egg,** symbol of the free-will offering made with the lamb; and **parsley,** a symbol of the green new growth that comes in the springtime.

The seder plate, often very ornate, is used only for the ritual part of the meal. It has a place of honor among the household's possessions. At the center of the table is a cup of wine known as Elijah's cup. It expresses a welcome for the prophet that Jews believe will herald the coming of the Messiah and the messianic age.

Earlier in the festivities, one of the three matzohs is divided in half, and a half is hidden while the children close their eyes. Toward the end of the meal, they search for the hidden half. Whoever finds it will exchange it for a promised gift. The half is then passed around for each person to take a piece. The eating of this piece of matzoh (known as *afikomen*—the Greek word for dessert) concludes the meal. No more food is served, though wine may be taken.

Though the Passover seder may last for several hours, it does not seem long because it is interspersed with the Exodus story, prayers, songs, blessings, a festive meal, and the companionship of loved ones. A final blessing brings the festivities to a close:

> The Passover service is now completed. With songs of praise we have lifted up the cup, symbolizing the divine promises of salvation, and we have called upon the Name of God. Let us again lift our souls to God in faith and hope. May He Who broke the Pharaoh's yoke, forever shatter all fetters of oppression and hasten the day when swords shall at last be broken and wars ended. Soon may He cause the glad tidings of redemption to be heard in all lands, so that mankind— freed from violence and from wrong and united in an eternal confidence of brotherhood—may celebrate the universal Passover in the Name of our God of Freedom.

SHAVUOT—THE FEAST OF WEEKS

Shavuot means "weeks" in Hebrew and is called the Feast of Weeks—because it occurs seven weeks after the second day of Passover—or Pentecost, the fiftieth day after Passover. It is observed on the sixth and seventh of Sivan. In ancient times it marked the conclusion of the grain harvest. It was one of the three pilgrimage festivals, a very joyous time. The people of a village would gather together and, with song and dance, go up to the Temple in Jerusalem to present to the Lord loaves of bread made from the finest wheat, and their first ripe fruits. It was and is a time to give thanks to the Lord for his goodness, to remind oneself to avoid greed and selfishness, and to remember that "not by bread alone shall man live, but by the word of God" (Dt 8:3).

In rabbinic times, when the Temple had been destroyed and there were no longer any pilgrimage festivals, Shavuot was transformed into a historical festival, commemorating the giving of the Torah to Moses on Mt. Sinai. This emphasis on revelation has enriched the festival of Shavuot and made it more spiritual.

The seven weeks from Passover to Shavuot link the two holidays. In fact, some ancient Jewish sources teach that Shavuot is the conclusion of Passover, since liberation is not complete without revelation.

Orthodox and Conservative Jews observe the festival for two days, Reform Jews for one day. One of the loveliest customs of Shavuot is the decorating of synagogues and homes with flowers and greens, symbolizing the mountain of Sinai.

A festive table is set, on which is served a meal of dairy products, such as cheesecakes and blintzes, milk, and honey—a reminder that the study of the Torah has the *"nourishment of milk and the sweetness of honey."* Triangular pancakes stuffed with cheese are favorites. They are triangular because the Torah

— is in three parts: Pentateuch, Prophets, and Writings;
— was given to a people of three parts: priests, Levites, and Israelites;
— was given in the third month through Moses, the third child of his parents.

Songs, hymns, and readings are a part of the ritual meal.

After the festive dinner on the eve of Shavuot, time is spent in study, either at home or in the synagogue, in preparation for the readings in the next morning's service. All Jews are supposed to regard themselves as actually receiving the Torah on Mt. Sinai.

What is the Torah? It is what God revealed to us and what we have come to understand about God. It is the ideas and ideals, the law and commandments that make up our religious heritage....It is the way of life, the path of self-fulfillment, the design for a better world....It is God's choicest gift to the House of Israel....Wherever people study the Torah, the Presence of God dwells among them.

(The preceding quotation is from the *New Union Prayer Book.* In a limited sense, the Torah comprises the first five books of the Bible, the Pentateuch, often referred to as The Five Books of Moses. In a broader sense, it applies to all the teaching of Judaism.)

The holidays we have discussed help Jews to remember and to relive the experiences that formed their religion and shaped them as a people. Most of these are rooted in the Bible and have been observed for many centuries. But Jews have also chosen to remember historic experiences in modern times that affected their destiny. Two in particular—the holocaust and the establishment of the State of Israel—have found a permanent place in the Jewish calendar.

Yom haShoah, or Holocaust Memorial Day, is observed on

the twenty-seventh day of Nisan (late April or early May). On that day or on the Sabbath closest to it, Jews gather in their synagogues to remember the greatest tragedy of their history, the loss of six million fellow Jews during the Second World War. One out of every two Jews in Europe—one third of the Jewish people in the entire world—was deliberately and systematically murdered during this terrible period, most in death camps that were set up by the Nazi regime as killing factories. Jews were shipped to these camps from every corner of Europe. They were men, women, and children. They posed no military threat; they were unarmed and nonviolent. Yet they were killed in terrible ways by the Nazis and their collaborators for one reason only, because they were Jews. Anti-Semitism—hatred of Jews and Judaism—had infected European culture for many years, and many people simply turned their backs on their Jewish neighbors. Since that great tragedy, Christian churches have condemned anti-Semitism as a sin against God and humanity, and some have criticized their own failure to defend and protect the Jewish people during the holocaust.

Yom haShoah is observed in various ways. Sometimes, stories or poems by holocaust survivors are read in the synagogue. Members of the congregation who lost relatives or friends are asked to stand and tell their names and their stories. They also recall and honor the righteous Christians who sheltered and saved Jews at great risk to their own lives and safety. The congregation ends the service by reciting the Kaddish, the traditional prayer for the dead. Some Christian churches have added a holocaust memorial service to their own church calendars in solidarity with the Jewish people. In some communities, there are interfaith services to commemorate the event.

If the holocaust is a reminder of what can happen to a people who have no homeland and no army to defend them, then *Yom haAtzma-ut,* Israel Independence Day, reminds Jews that there is now a Jewish homeland. Following less than two weeks after commemoration of the sad and tragic losses of the holocaust, Israel Independence Day allows Jews to rejoice in the reestablishment of their ancient homeland as an independent, sovereign, and democratic Jewish commonwealth after nearly two thousand years. Israel declared itself a nation on May 15, 1948, and maintained its independence through a number of wars and attacks from hostile Arab nations, and bombings and murders inside its borders by terrorist groups opposed to peace or recognition. In recent years, Israel has made peace with two of its Arab neighbors, Egypt and Jordan, and also has established formal diplomatic ties with the Vatican. On the Jewish calendar, Israel Independence Day is observed on the fifth day of Iyar (late April or early May).

While Israel Independence Day is not a religious holy day, there is usually a synagogue service on that day or the Sabbath closest to it, which includes a prayer for the State of Israel, asking God to provide wisdom and guidance to its leaders and peace and contentment within its borders. (American Jews offer a similar prayer for their own country, for the people and leaders of the United States during the high holy days).

Holocaust Memorial Day and Israel Independence Day are two more examples of the importance of memory in Jewish tradition.

Chapter 6

Judaism's Influence on Christianity

"Our Father Who art in heaven, hallowed be Thy name...." This prayer, often called the Lord's Prayer, is acknowledged by the majority of Christians to be one of the simplest and most beautiful prayers in all the world's religious literature—a prayer we look upon as being original with Our Lord. And so it is in its choice of ideas, in their grouping, in the simple, beautiful language used. But it is thoroughly Jewish in its content. Each of the petitions can be found in the prayers of Jewish liturgies—prayers Our Lord himself would have said many, many times. Sometimes we forget that Jesus was a Jew, faithful to Jewish law and teaching. Mary and Joseph were faithful Jews. The apostles and disciples, the first Christians, were Jews, attending the meetings in the synagogues, worshiping in the Temple, fulfilling Jewish laws and customs. These first followers of Jesus were tolerated as a sect within the Jewish community. Judaism in the decades before the uprising against Rome was so divided into parties and sects that one more did not pose a problem. The trouble began when more and more Gentiles joined the Jewish followers of Christ.

In the Acts of the Apostles we read that Peter and Paul argued as to whether or not Gentiles converting to Christ should be required to follow the Mosaic Law. The decision was that they were not. As a result, Christians lost the sense of their Judaic background down through the centuries. However, since the earliest followers of Christ saw themselves as a part *of* not apart *from* Judaism, when the break came they took with them many of the essential elements of Judaism:

- *Belief in One God.* The essential belief that all recognize as coming to us through the Jewish people is the belief in *one* God. God revealed himself to Abram, entrusted to him knowledge about himself, and gave him the task of passing on that truth to his descendants. God changed Abram's name to Abraham, which means "father of many nations." ("No longer shall your name be Abram, you shall be called Abraham, the father of a multitude of nations" [Gn 17:4].) It is from him that the Jewish people descended. The one sentence that sums up Jewish faith is the opening sentence from the Sh'ma (Shema): "Hear, O Israel, the Lord our God, the Lord is one." It is this belief in one God that set the Israelites apart from all other peoples. Clinging to this belief has caused much hardship and suffering—even death—for the Jews.

- *People as Made in the Image and Likeness of God.* Another belief of utmost importance to us is that each individual is made in the image and likeness of God. The Jews do not claim this for themselves alone. They teach that *each* person is created by God in his image and likeness. What a different world we would have if we stopped to realize what it means to be created in God's image and likeness! The infinite worth of each person! *Each* of us has the *right* to the love, the respect, and the care of every person. This right imposes on *us* the *responsibility* to respect, love, and care for *every* person. The rabbis teach that to save the life of a single person is like saving the entire universe, and to destroy the life of a single person is like destroying the entire universe.

- ***The Bible.*** Hebrew Scriptures make up the core of what we used to call the Old Testament. When we read from it, our instruction and inspiration come from Jewish sources. Often, Christians have considered the Hebrew Scriptures as portraying God as harsh and vindictive as opposed to the God of love preached by Christ. But when Christ was asked which of the commandments was the greatest, he answered: *"Love the Lord your God with your whole heart, your whole soul, and your whole mind"* (from Deuteronomy 6:5) and: *"The second is like unto this: 'Love your neighbor as yourself'"* (from Leviticus 19:18). The Torah is a law of love. *Torah* means "teaching," not "law" in our sense of the word. In Jewish teaching and prayers, along with the awesomeness of God and his demand for justice, are found many references to God as a loving Father, a merciful God. You may have heard the saying: *"An eye for an eye, a tooth for a tooth."* It is not the harsh law we so often consider it to be. The Jewish leaders introduced that law to mitigate the excessive and unjust punishment meted out to people in ancient times for petty crimes. One's life could be forfeited for a simple theft. The Jewish leaders insisted that no more could be exacted of a person than what he had done. They even went further in interpreting that law. A person need not actually be required to lose an eye or limb because of having destroyed the eye or limb of another. He or she could have the option of repaying the victim in a monetary way or by providing the necessary service to the individual that would recompense the victim for the injury.

The Ten Commandments that Christians and many other religious denominations observe as norms for living one's life are found in Exodus, the second book of the Bible (20:1-18). God gave the Ten Commandments to Moses for the Jewish people and through them to us.

Even the New Testament is permeated with Jewish thought, since most of it was written by Jews. The seeming conflict and controversies between the Christian Jews and the non-Christian Jews in the New Testament result from misinterpretations and misunderstandings.

In speaking about the Hebrew Scriptures in an address given for the Center for Jewish and Christian Learning at the College of St. Thomas, St. Paul, Minnesota, Joseph Cardinal Bernardin said:

A growing number of Catholic exegetes have come to a better understanding of the richness of the first part of the Bible and a deeper appreciation of how these writings had positively influenced the teachings of Jesus and early Christianity....We are recognizing, however slowly, that, without deep immersion into the spirit and texts of the Hebrew Scriptures, Christians experience an emaciated version of Jesus' full religious vision.

• ***The Sabbath.*** It is from the Jews that we received the concept of a day set aside each week to worship God—to share in the "rest of God"—and to acknowledge God as absolute Master by refraining from work, allowing for physical and spiritual renewal. The Sabbath became and remains one of the most important signs of the covenant between God and his people. Jews observe the Sabbath on Saturday, the seventh day of the week—the day on which God rested. For Christians, the greatest and most important event in all history, the Resurrection of Christ, occurred on Sunday, the first day of the week. Therefore, Christians observe the Sabbath on Sunday.

- **The Church.** Churches or neighborhood centers for religious worship as we know them today did not exist in ancient times. Religious centers were located in the city that served as the seat of government, as was the great Temple of the Jews in Jerusalem. However, when the first Jewish Temple was destroyed in 586 B.C. and the Jews were taken into exile in Babylon, they felt a need to come together on the Sabbath to praise God and study the Torah as well as to keep their identity and to hold on to their customs. As time went on, these regular gatherings developed an organized format and continued even after the restoration of the Temple. The term *synagogue,* which, like *ecclesia,* means "a gathering of people," became synonymous with the building where the gatherings took place—just as church is so often thought of as the building where worshipers meet to pray. The early followers of Christ were accustomed to meeting in the synagogue for prayer and study each Sabbath. When they broke with Jewish tradition, they continued the practice, but met on Sunday in their homes and, later, in churches.

- **The Office.** The Office, the daily prayer of the church, is made up of prayers, psalms, and hymns, very similar to the synagogue service. Priests and cloistered religious (priests, brothers, and sisters who do not leave their monasteries or convents unless necessary) say the Divine Office. This is the full Office divided into segments that are said at definite hours throughout the day and night. A shorter version of the Office is said by many congregations of religious who are in active ministries (for example, teaching, nursing, and social work). The custom of saying the morning portion of the Office, morning prayer, before daily mass has been introduced in many parishes.

- *Grace at Meals.* Our custom of saying grace before and after meals comes to us from the Jews. Jewish meals are prefaced with benedictions; readings and hymns may accompany the eating and drinking, especially in ritual meals. A prayer of thanksgiving follows the meal.

- *Pentecost (Shavuot).* Pentecost comes fifty days after the second day of Passover in Judaism and fifty days after Easter in Christianity. *Pentecost* means "fifty days." It celebrates for both religious communities the founding of the people of God. For Jews it recalls the giving of the Torah on Mt. Sinai, and for Christians the descent of the Holy Spirit in the form of tongues of fire upon the apostles and those at prayer with them.

- *The Altar, Vestments, Reading Table or Lectern, Sanctuary Lamp, Use of Incense.* All come from Jewish practice.

- *The Mass.* The format of the mass, especially the liturgy of the word with its readings from Scripture, follows much the same format as that of the synagogue service. It also parallels, to some extent, the Passover seder in the liturgy of the eucharist.

    - *Entrance Antiphon*–gathers the people for worship.

    - *The Gloria*–parallels the canticles or hymns of praise from the Hebrew Scriptures used in the synagogue service.

    - *The Psalms*–are sung by the cantor in the synagogue service and by the leader of song (if there is one) in the mass. If no leader of song is present, the psalm is recited by the congregation.

— *The Gospel Procession*—The reader, accompanied by servers bearing candles, bringing the lectionary to the pulpit is like the procession of the rabbi or reader bringing the Torah from the ark to the reading table.

— *The Homily*—The explanation of the Scriptures read at mass is like the rabbi's homily in the synagogue service.

— *Prayers at the Blessing of the Bread and Wine* (at the offertory)—are like the prayers used at Sabbath meals.

— *The Washing of Hands*—is a purification of self in preparation for the offering of sacrifice to God just as the priests did in Temple times.

— *The "Holy, Holy, Holy Lord"* (Preface)—is from Isaiah and is said in Jewish worship.

— *The Final Blessing*—given by the priest as father of a faith family at the end of mass is much like the Jewish father's blessing given to his children as they left home in ancient times.

· ***The Teachings of Jesus.*** Chapters 2 and 3 of Dr. Eugene Fisher's book *Faith Without Prejudice* (Paulist Press) contain an excellent summary of the Jewish background of Christ's teaching. He tells us that the ever-challenging message of Christ

to be understood, must be seen as rooted in the history and religious convictions of His people, the Jews. Jesus considered Himself to be a faithful Jew. He observed the Jewish law, the Torah, and cherished it as the inspired Word of God....He also used the teaching methods of the rabbis of His time. He acted and taught in the manner of the Pharisees, who represented the common classes—the aristocratic Sadducees represented the monied classes....Jesus was given the title of "rabbi" by the people of His time, which indicated that they viewed Him as a Pharisee.

Certainly, Jesus sided with the group of Pharisees who depended on and humanized the teachings of the Torah, stressing love, loyalty, and compassion. To quote Father John Pawlikowski in his *Catechetics and Prejudice* (Paulist Press),

Extending hospitality to the traveler, visiting the sick of all religious groups, giving charity anonymously, burying the dead, helping to bring peace to those who lack it: these duties were never clearly set forth in the Hebrew Bible, although they were generally felt in spirit. The rabbis (Pharisees) fashioned such duties into new commandments which highlighted the role of prayer over sacrifice, and gave each person in Israel a priestly function.

From the doctrines of the Pharisees come the beliefs in the resurrection of the dead, heaven and hell, angels, and the last judgment. Not all Jews believe in bodily resurrection. But, because we are made in the image and likeness of God, that image and likeness, often referred to as the soul, cannot cease to exist. What happens to the soul after the death of the body is not clear. Some Jews believe, as we do, that the souls of those who led a life in accordance with God's law will be rewarded in heaven. The souls of those who refused to obey God's law will go to hell. Descriptions of heaven and hell are pure speculation. Just what heaven and hell are like is not known.

This is a brief—very brief—summary of the wealth we have received from Judaism—an appreciation of what we owe to the Jewish people, the chosen people of God, the covenanted people, whose covenant has never been revoked by God.

It is good to learn and rejoice in what we as Christians (especially Roman Catholics) have in common with the Jews and people of other faiths, but, as Father John Pawlikowski (a recognized authority in interfaith relations) has often remarked in ecumenical and interfaith meetings: "We must also celebrate our differences."

A major difference in the beliefs between Christians and Jews is the doctrine of the Trinity. From the time of Abraham, the Jews have believed in and stressed that God is *one*. It is stated in the Sh'ma, the prayer that all pious Jews pray three times a day: "Hear, O Israel, the Lord our God, the Lord is one." Christ's revelation that the one, true God is a triune God was and is unacceptable to Jews. For them the concept of a human being equal to God and incarnate in human form constitutes blasphemy. The more the church has developed the doctrine of the Incarnation, acknowledging Christ to be divine, calling him the Second Person of the Trinity—Father, Son, and Holy Spirit—the greater has grown the barrier between Christians and Jews. Another major difference is the belief that Jesus is the Christ, the Greek word for the Messiah. For Jews, the Messiah was to inaugurate a messianic age of peace. The whole universe would acknowledge the one God, the Creator, the Lord of Israel. He would reassemble his people in their own land, and all sorrow and suffering would cease. None of this was evident when Christ came. *Seemingly*, he had not changed the course of history. The messianic age had not come; therefore, he could not be the awaited Messiah.

Dr. Eva Fleischner, a Roman Catholic theologian and former professor of religion at Montclair State College, New Jersey, in one of her public lectures said:

In its essence messianic hope, Christian as much as Jewish, is rooted in the vision of a great future; in the belief that God is Lord of history and that, therefore, history is going somewhere, is moving to a climax, a transformation, a glorious future. Something unimaginably wonderful and great is yet to come. This consummation of all things will be the work of God, although human beings can hasten its coming by the way in which they live their lives. For Christians it is associated with the Person of Christ....Regardless of our theological views, we are meant to make this earth into a world of justice and peace.

This is our task, and, in endeavoring to build bridges between peoples of different faiths—bridges that join us in a common effort to build God's kingdom here on earth without losing our identity, our freedom to be ourselves—we have begun to accomplish it.

scribe

Appendix A:
Some Famous Jews in
American History

Abraham ben Samuel Zacuto. One of six Jews in Columbus' crew of ninety. His astronomical tables guided Columbus through the uncharted seas.

Haym Salomon. A member of the Sons of Liberty, a supportive organization of the Revolution. He raised $200,000 to help finance the Revolutionary cause.

Isaac Moses. Helped the cause of the Revolutionary War by lending money to the government.

Levi Strauss. Merchant, banker, philanthropist and creator of a clothing empire that still thrives. Levi's is one of the most popular brand names known in the world.

Ernestine Rose. After twelve years of campaigning for a bill to grant married women the right to own property, she won a legal victory that sparked the beginning of the National Women's Rights Movement.

Emma Lazarus. American-Jewish poet and essayist. "The New Colossus"—a sonnet that appears on the base of the Statue of Liberty welcoming immigrants to American shores—was written by her.

The New Colossus

Not like the brazen giant of Greek fame
with conquering limbs astride from land to land,
Here at our sea-washed, sunset gates shall stand
A mighty woman with a torch, whose fame
Is the imprisoned lightning, and her name
Mother of Exiles, from her beacon-hand
Glows world-wide welcome; her mild eyes command
The air-bridged harbor that twin cities frame,
"Keep, ancient lands, your storied pomp," she cried
with silent lips. "Give me your tired, your poor,
Your huddled masses yearning to breathe free,
The wretched refuse of your teeming shore,
Send these, the homeless, tempest-tost to me.
I lift my lamp beside the Golden Door!"

This tablet, with her sonnet to the Bartholdi Statue of Liberty engraved upon it, is placed upon these walls in loving memory of

EMMA LAZARUS

Born in New York City, July 22nd 1849. Died November 19th, 1887.

Samuel Gompers. Labor leader and founder of the AF of L.

Guggenheim Family. Industrialists and philanthropists. Solomon Guggenheim (1856-1930) endowed the Guggenheim Museum for Modern Art in New York City.

Henry Kissinger. Secretary of state under President Nixon.

Herbert Lehman. Governor of New York.

Henry Morgenthau. Cabinet member; secretary of the Treasury.

Joseph Pulitzer. Editor and publisher. Founder of the Pulitzer Prizes—the highest annual literary award in the United States.

Abraham A. Ribicoff. Cabinet member, senator, and governor of Connecticut.

Hyman Rickover. Admiral and head of the atomic submarine project.

Julius Rosenwald. Founder of Sears, Roebuck & Company.

Stage and Screen Stars. Woody Allen, George Burns, Eddie Cantor, Aaron Copland, Dustin Hoffman, Al Jolson, the Marx Brothers, Dinah Shore, Beverly Sills, Barbra Streisand.

Musicians. Irving Berlin, Leonard Bernstein, Walter Damrosch, Bob Dylan, George Gershwin, Jascha Heifetz, Vladimir Horowitz, Jerome Kern, Yehudi Menuhin, Itzhak Perlman, Richard Rodgers.

Movie Producers. William Fox, Samuel Goldwyn, the Warner Brothers.

Scientists. Albert Einstein (Nobel Prize winner), Jonas E. Salk (discovered the polio vaccine, which helped to virtually eliminate the crippling disease).

Athletes. Hank Greenberg, Sandy Koufax, Sid Luckman, Mark Spitz.

Authors and Playwrights. Edna Ferber, Fannie Hurst, Arthur Miller, Herman Wouk.

First Woman Rabbi. Sally J. Priesand.

Out of 621 ***Nobel Prize winners,*** 82 were Jewish.

The preceding list of famous Jews is by no means complete. Perhaps you can add to the list.

_____

_____

_____

_____

_____

_____

Appendix B:
Bibliography

Frank, Anne. *Diary of a Young Girl.* New York: Knopf, 1994.

Meir, Golda. *My Life.* New York: Putnam, 1975.

Potok, Chaim. *The Book of Lights.* New York: Random House, 1981.

———. *The Chosen.* New York: Simon & Schuster, 1967.

———. *My Name Is Asher Lev.* New York: Knopf, 1972.

———. *The Promise.* New York: Knopf, 1969.

———. *Wanderings (History of the Jews).* New York: Knopf, 1978.

Singer, Isaac B. *Gimpel the Fool.* New York: Noonday Books, 1957.

———. *The Magician of Lublin.* New York: Noonday Books, 1960.

———. *The Penitent.* New York: Farrar, Straus, Giroux, 1983.

———. *The Spinoza of Market Street.* New York: Farrar, Straus, Giroux, 1961.

———. *Stories for Children.* New York: Farrar, Straus, Giroux, 1984.

Wiesel, Elie. *The Accident.* New York: Hill & Wang, 1972.

———. *Dawn.* New York: Hill & Wang, 1972.

——. *Gates of the Forest.* New York: Holt, Rinehart & Winston, 1966.

——. *Night.* New York: Hill & Wang, 1972.

——. *The Town Beyond the Wall.* New York: Holt, Rinehart & Winston, 1964.